The Spirit of
RURAL AUSTRALIA

The Spirit of
RURAL AUSTRALIA

WORDS BY LIAM DAVISON   PHOTOGRAPHY BY JIM CONQUEST

NH
NEW
HOLLAND

Published in Australia in 1999 by
New Holland Publishers (Australia) Pty Ltd
Sydney • Auckland • London • Cape Town
14 Aquatic Drive Frenchs Forest NSW 2086 Australia
1A/218 Lake Road Northcote Auckland New Zealand
24 Nutford Place London W1H 6DQ United Kingdom
80 McKenzie Street Cape Town 8001 South Africa

National Library of Australia Cataloguing-in-Publication Data:

Davison, Liam, 1957- .
The spirit of rural Australia.

ISBN 1 86436 439 9.

1. Farm life – Australia. 2. Farm life – Australia – Pictorial works. 3. Australia – Rural conditions.
4. Australia – Rural conditions – Pictorial works. I. Conquest, Jim. II. Title.

630.994

Publishing General Manager: Jane Hazell
Publisher: Averill Chase
Designer: Kerry Klinner
Editor: Emma Wise
Printer: Imago Productions, Singapore

Front cover: Milk separator, Coolart.
Back cover: Old mill interior, Kyneton.
Title page: Shea, Linda and Tammy Carney.
Foreword: Vineyard, Main Ridge.

ACKNOWLEDGMENTS

We would like to acknowledge the following people for their help and encouragement with this book:
Julia, Jacqueline, Daniel-Rory and Clare Conquest, Francesca Davison, Garry Holzworth, Leonie Lavell, Patchy Mitchell,
Lizzy Gannon, Frank Hoban, and Brendan and Grace Flynn. Also, Kerry Klinner, Emma Wise and Averill Chase
for their untiring work in bringing it all together.

For my parents, Jack and Liz Conquest.

J.C.

For Frankie, Sam and Milly.

L.D.

CONTENTS

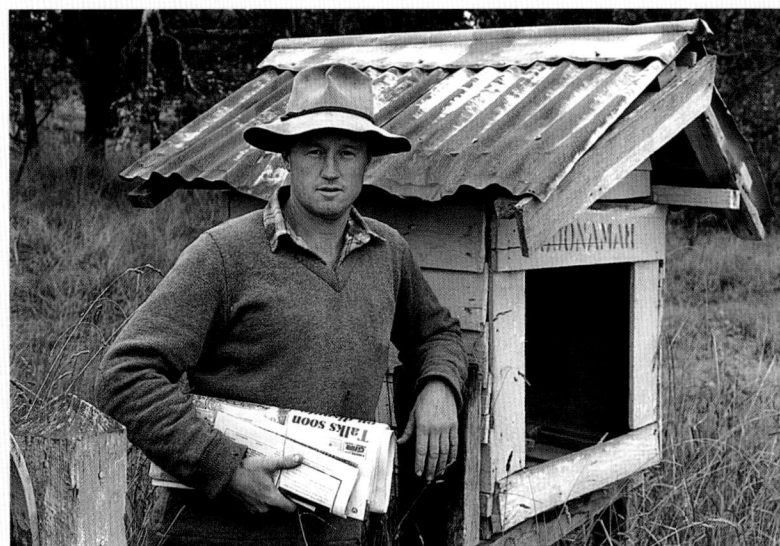

INTRODUCTION

◆

THE SHAPE AND PATTERN
OF THE LAND

Not far from where I live there is a stretch of land on the north facing slope of a small valley. From the top of the rise, you look out across three hectares of corrugated vines to a small creek, then on to rolling pasture with a dark bank of pines in the distance. The vines have been in for five and a half years, long enough to stake their claim. Late in the season their red leaves spill like a wine stain across the hill. The trellises come to an abrupt halt by a stretched wire fence where the knuckled branches of unpruned apples scratch skyward.

Thirty years ago, this was prime apple and pear country. Nine thousand acres of trees produced more than a million cases of fruit per year. The pasture on the far side of the valley is the legacy of classic top-dressed rye and subterranean clover. Introduced in the 1920s for sheep and cattle, it is rich and lush,

so brilliantly green it almost hurts your eyes to look. When the first pastoral leases were taken out in the 1840s, the valley was lightly wooded with messmate and manna gum. Stock was fed on native grass. The dark pines, now looking more like a heavy bruise on the far slope than a row of trees, were planted as windbreaks in the 1860s when the squatting runs were broken into smaller selections. They mark the original boundary

In 1801, the crew of the Lady Nelson slid a worn shovel into the soft earth to cultivate a small plot on the lee of the island. They planted English wheat and corn. They pushed peach stones and apple seeds into the newly opened ground. When the ship returned six months later, the first harvest yielded a bushel of corn from the flourishing garden.

This book explores the relationship forged between the land and the people who work it. The imprint of that first shovel foreshadowed the monumental process of change that transformed rural Australia over the following 200 years. Pastoralism and agriculture, horticulture and mixed farming, orchards and vineyards—all have left their mark. As have land-clearance and pasture improvement programs and integrated approaches to land management. All have contributed to the shape and pattern of a land which changes as we watch.

Our past is still with us, not least in the physical legacy of town or fence or early home. This book explores rural Australia through these records of a period which has seen the land transformed many times over through its simultaneous exposure to agrarian and technological revolutions. It also explores the constants in this changing environment—the pleasing ache at the end of a hard day's work, the cold metallic taste of water from the tank, the sight of long awaited rain sweeping in across the paddocks. As rural Australia welcomes and embraces change, farmers still lean against

between properties selected sight unseen from survey maps in town and systematically cleared for pasture.

Piled logs and post-and-rail fences stamped the first straight lines on the land—lines that persist in furrow, orchard, road and trellis now. Follow one of these lines through the corrugated paddock of young vines, down the slope to the trickling creek and along it to its mouth. There, on the far side of the tidal flats of Westernport Bay is Churchill Island, the site of the first garden planted in Victoria.

saleyard rails catching up on news. They still rise with the sparrows, keep a watchful eye on the weather and leave their boots by the kitchen door.

THE CHATTER
OF METAL WHEELS

If you look inside an average machine shed on one of Australia's older rural properties, you are likely to find an overwhelming tangle of disused ploughs and harvesters, tractors and engines, chaffcutters and binders. You are also likely to find the clean lines of the sophisticated machinery currently in use. This clutter of discarded agricultural implements, so often surprising to overseas visitors, bears witness to the enthusiasm of people on the land for the new—new technologies, buildings, crops and pastures as well as new work practices and approaches to land management. Rural Australia is anything but complacent about change.

In 1883, a year after their invention, 43 combined reaping and binding machines were displayed at the Numurkah Agricultural Show in northern Victoria. By the following year, 787 were listed in Victoria alone. By 1890, there were five times that number. Four stripper harvesters which incorporated winnowing were available between 1884 and 1886 for farmers in drier regions. One thousand were produced by H.V. McKay at Sunshine for the 1920 harvest

which was brought in to the thwack of belts and the chatter of metal wheels driving the great combs through the paddocks.

Similar developments occurred with ploughs and seed drills, scarifiers and cultivators. The number of horses used on Victorian farms to power the new machines more than doubled between 1881 and 1912. A typical Australian stripper harvester with a 10-foot cut required five horses to pull it.

Across the land, the steady tread of horses drove the country forward. Saddle and spur, bit and bridle, harness and brace. A farrier and forge in every country town.

All was to change with the rumbling arrival of the traction engine. These great-bellied machines, with their thumping strength and relentless dreadnought wheels, pounded the way clear for the more efficient tractor. 'Big Lizzie', a huge road traction engine built in 1915, stomped its way for two years from Melbourne to Mildura, scaring the horses and heralding the arrival of a new age.

By the end of World War I, the tractor was here to stay. McKay and McDonald manufactured them locally throughout the 1920s and, slowly but steadily, the rural landscape was transformed. Horses remained important, but farmers were quick to recognise the benefits of a machine which ate only while it worked. By 1930, the number of horses in use on farms had dropped by 25 per cent while the number of tractors had more than tripled. More and more farmers learned the secrets of the magneto and the cleated wheel. They worked to the steady throb of the Imperial E-B tractor and the whiff of kerosene.

And it wasn't only tractors. Milking machines breathed in dairies. Mechanical separators hummed. By 1930 the district butter factory had all but replaced the small farm dairy. Refrigerated cool stores extended the life of fruit. Electricity filled the sheds with dazzling light. Pumps and windmills beat like hearts. The rhythmic click and whisper of blades through wool gave way to the din of spindle-driven cutters. By 1911, fifty thousand Wolseley machines were shearing eighty million sheep a year.

Change today is quieter but just as rapid. A farmer is as likely to invest in a computer as a tractor. Laser technology is reshaping the land as comprehensively as the traction engine and wrought steel ploughshares. The laboratory brings more

WOODEN FENCES, EUROPEAN TREES

With first settlement, pastoralists and graziers moved onto land that had been carefully managed for thousands of years. The sparse forests and open parkland so often remarked upon by early settlers were not so much formed by nature as through careful attention to what the land could sustain by the Aboriginal people who had lived in close association with it for thousands of years. It was a land that had never been fenced; a land that had never felt the tread of cloven hooves or the penetration of a metal plough.

Despite the shortage of skilled farmers and agricultural implements in Australia's early years, free settlers soon took advantage of the land's potential for improvement. In Victoria alone, seven million acres of freehold land had been claimed by 1850, the European pattern of land management stamped upon it. Straight lines, wooden fences, European trees. Roads and stock routes linking isolated settlements. Gradually, the unmistakeable grid pattern of European expansion was imprinted on the ancient land. Gradually, the land itself changed colour, taking on the hues of wheat and barley, oats and clover.

With these came other lasting changes. Improvement meant making it more like home. Rabbits and foxes were sprung from traps for sport. Blackberries were scattered on the

change than the factory or forge. For people on the land today, market and crop projections, weather analyses and paddock profiles are just as valuable to the business of farming as the harvester or hoe. Little wonder then, that you are just as likely to find today's farmers attending rural seminars to keep abreast of new developments as you are to see them walking the land or checking stock.

wind. Elms and oaks dropped their European leaves each winter. A great proliferation of native trees trailed in the wake of the settled lands in response to the European fear of fire, sometimes taking root in places they had never been known before. Thick scrub that would later demand to be cleared encroached upon once open space.

Chinese gardeners terraced the silted creeks and tidal flats with vegetables and filled the valleys with tobacco. They paddied rice and pricked the northern states with pineapples. By the end of the 19th century, three quarters of the vegetables eaten in Australia came from Chinese gardens. No plot of land was too small for planting. German and Italian settlers trellised the broad acres with vines and groved the hills with olives. They planted walnuts, hazels, peaches, plums; they fenced and cellared the new land; they walled and built.

Smaller holdings brought tighter networks of roads and fences to the patterned land. Four kilometres of post and rail is needed to enclose a 320-acre selection. Three kilometres of knotted wire to a paddocked acre. A ton of dry-stacked stone for each fenced metre. Strung or hedged or post-and-railed—the land was blocked and sectioned off.

More than a million acres of new land came under cultivation between 1861 and 1880 in response to the Land Selection Acts which broke up the larger leases. There were 206 000 farms in Australia by the middle of this century. Migration and massive British investment in the wool industry vastly increased Australia's rural population. Here was a new land ripe for improvement by resident smallhold farmers.

'Closer Settlement' schemes, linked with land reclamation and irrigation projects, changed the pattern

all directions they headed for town, lifting the dust with horse and truck and ute as they carried in their news. The mail routes spidered out again, circling the divided acres, while the slung wires of the telephone looped from pole to pole. The proliferation of country towns had as much to do with shaping a rural identity as the clearing of the paddocks.

THE PATTERN CHANGES

Just as the circumstances of Australia's settlement and its early development as a rural economy exposed people on the land to more rapid change than that felt by their counterparts elsewhere, the current generation of Australian farmers have faced some of the greatest challenges. The rural landscape has changed dramatically over the last forty years or so in response to deregulation of the Australian market and

again. Swamps were drained. Deserts flourished. Ditches and canals shone with glistening water. Rows of fruit trees blossomed in the heat. Scrub was raked and burned, often for days on end till the countryside was blanketed with a pall of smoke. Dry farming brought new shoots from the dust to turn the brown land green. New strains of wheat and the powdered fall of phosphate kept the towering silos full.

All across Australia stock moved from farm to saleyard, and produce passed from orchard to cool store, shed to mill. Wooden wheels rutted the hard earth until tracks and paths developed into roads. Farm was linked to farm, station to station. Where roads crossed, clusters of buildings developed into towns. A pub and general store, a church and sportsground. A pussy-willowed school. Stock and station agents beside the public hall. A place for the district to gather. Sales days, church and sport. Telegraph, post and bank. From

monumental shifts in world economies. In particular, Britain's entry into the Common Market in the early 1970s and her more recent involvement with the European Union have forced farmers to develop new specialised markets, particularly in Asia, and to operate even more competitively than they have in the past. Subsidised American produce has not made their task any easier.

Not surprisingly, the same spirit of resilience and resourcefulness that characterised earlier rural communities enables today's farmers to embrace change creatively as a necessary part of progress. New markets for wheat, wool and beef have been established in China and Japan. More intensive farming methods have been introduced to cater for specific market needs like grain-fed beef and pork. Our dairy industry has turned more confidently towards South-East Asia.

If deregulation has brought hardship for many on the land, it has also opened the way for new ventures with the potential to vastly increase Australia's export market. Cotton farming, which started with small plantations in the prime cattle and sheep country of northern New South Wales in the 1960s, is now one of our major export industries. Relatively free from government regulation and the effects of trade wars between the United States and European Union, both of which have hindered wool and wheat exports in recent years, cotton farmers have been quick to establish lucrative market connections with Japan, Taiwan, Korea and South-East Asia. It is an exciting frontier industry open to big corporate investors as well as family farmers.

Large plantations of olives and almonds in the Riverina reflect a similar diversification in fruit growing regions across the country. While some growers turn towards new crops,

others are uprooting older, less productive orchards in favour of new, heavy-cropping plantings. Wheat growers are turning to new strains such as high protein durum for the local pasta market.

Investment incentives have also created new opportunities in the revitalised Australian wine industry which is dramatically increasing its share of the export market. The Rutherglen–Sunraysia regions of Victoria increased their grape intake six times over between 1960 and 1980. New grape varieties and wine regions and the development of specialist wineries in tourist areas reflect the ongoing confidence in an industry known for the quality of its product and its potential for expansion.

As new crops, markets and farming methods are being developed in response to Australia's unprecedented exposure to world economic crises, the conversion to broadacre farming and bulk handling technology has placed more land under the plough than ever before with consistently high yields. Farmers, ever sensitive to the land they work, are keenly aware of associated issues of sustainability, especially as this relates to intensive farming practice. In the early 1970s, almost one million tonnes of superphosphate was spread each year in Victoria alone. The use of pesticides was just as liberal. Nowadays, computerised farm management systems monitor and control the volumes used and you are just as likely to find farmers employing alternative methodologies like organic pest control and continuous cropping or minimum tillage techniques to maintain soil quality. Paddocks cleared more than a hundred years ago are slowly changing colour again as

tree planting programs and soil conservation works undo some of the damage done by earlier excesses.

Such change has a lasting effect on rural communities. The trend towards smaller holdings has been reversed in recent years. Government, banks and industry leaders have encouraged farmers to expand in response to market forces. By the early 1990s, the 206 000 farms registered in Australia in 1955 had been reduced to 126 000. While the majority of these are still family owned, the shift to larger farms and smaller numbers of workers has forced a reassessment of how business is done on the land. Smaller rural townships, especially those relying on single staples, were still viable as late as the 1970s or 1980s. Now, they too are feeling the pinch as improved amenities draw people to larger rural centres. Again, the pattern is changing.

A way of life that we might once have assumed was an inviolable part of our national heritage is slowly being transformed. It leaves behind familiar landmarks. Fences, houses, public buildings, clearings and plantations. Machinery and tools, domestic appliances. All speak to us of a past that is still close. Through them, and through the land itself, we connect with the communities on which our own are built and recognise ourselves.

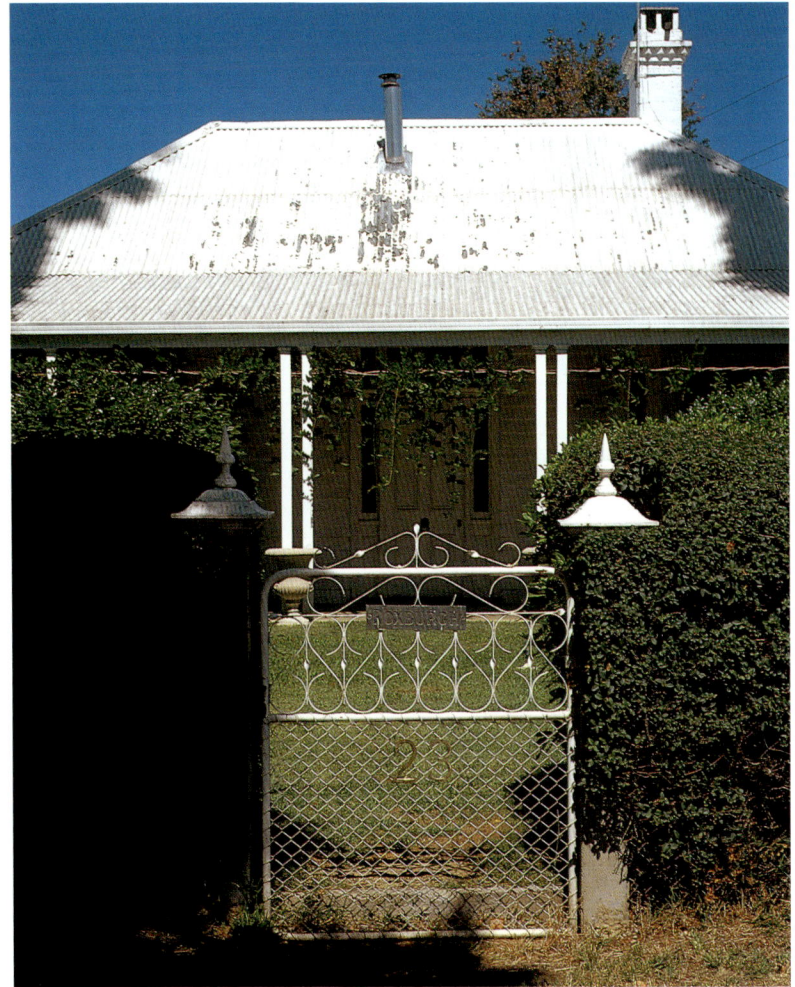

Even as we accept the inevitable process of change that keeps us moving into the future, we see how much things stay the same. This book explores the presence of the past through images and words that reflect our changing relationship with the land in a celebration of the resilient spirit of rural Australia.

LAND

LAND

AUSTRALIA HAS BEEN A MAJOR agricultural exporter for more than a century, and those who work closely with the land know we are still learning to understand this country we claim as our own. Three hundred million years ago, much of Australia was covered by ice. Since then, volcanic upheavals and erosion have helped produce the land of worn plains and ancient mountain ranges we know today, leaving a relatively thin covering of nutrient-deficient soil. Such conditions demand carefully implemented land-management principles and a particular sensitivity to the environment being worked.

Productivity has not come easily—right from the start, European settlers recognised the need to adapt familiar farming practice to the specific needs of the new land. Watkin Tench, who arrived with the First Fleet, reported that after three years of back-breaking effort on the land: 'A spot eminently fruitful has never been discovered. There are many spots cursed with everlasting and unconquerable sterility…Provided a sufficient number of cattle be imported to afford manure for dressing the ground, no doubt can exist that subsistence may be drawn from it.'

Unlike earlier observers such as Cook, who reported a land where 'grain, fruits, roots etc. of every kind would flourish,' Tench recognised the enormous investment needed to reap this country's rewards. Today, 33 per cent of agricultural land in Australia has been treated with trace element supplements. Millions of tonnes of superphosphate are spread on Australian soil each year.

Increasingly, Australian farmers and Landcare organisations are recognising the fragility of Australia's ecosystems and the need to manage the land in ways that cater to its specific needs. Tree planting, soil conservation and water management schemes work hand in hand with increasing crop diversification and the development of new strains of seed and animal breeds to bring about farming methods best suited to the land itself.

Much of the early enthusiasm for what the land might offer stemmed from an inability to see the country for what it was. The open, park-like tracts of land remarked upon by early explorers were the direct result of at least 40 000 years of careful land management by the Aborigines who had developed a sustainable way of life through close association with the land. Fire was used as a sophisticated agricultural tool. Permanent stone weirs and fish-traps were built at the mouths of rivers.

It is not difficult to see the influence we have had on this land since European settlement and how we have shaped it to our needs. Thousands of hectares have been cleared and fenced for agriculture. Streams have been diverted and unproductive land improved. But the land has shaped us also. Its nature has determined our patterns of settlement, our crops and diet, a distinctive style of housing and architecture and a sense of aesthetics that is reflected in our literature and art. An increasing awareness of the need for long-term sustainability is still influencing the way we work. People on the land who look to the next generation know better than most that the land claims us as absolutely as we claim it.

STRINGING THE
PADDOCKS

All day, he has strung the paddocks tight, listening to the knotted wire as it stutters from the spool. Post to post, he has drawn the line, feeling the tension mount. A good fence works both ways. It lays claim and strains against the ground that holds it. Each turn pulls it taut till the sixty acres vibrates like an instrument.

He drags it to himself, marks out his family's future with the twisted wire—this hill, this stand of gums, this gently falling slope—claiming the years ahead as though he is baling hay. Each metre throws its pricked shadow out across the land: three sharp lines with each bar measured by a post. Each long hour stretches his own shadow larger as he reels his future in.

He braces himself against the heart rail and keeps on working. Nip and splice, stretch and staple. When he lifts his head he sees how far he's come: the straight length of it, and the measured knots marking out his years.

NET WORK

It starts with water weeping through stone. High above him on the granite slope begins the slow descent. It slides and trickles, finds a course, builds to creek and tributary and stream, each new outfall plaiting the tea-brown water like muscles in a forearm. He knows each bank and shoal, each stony weir; knows each sweeping curve of this, his river. Every drop of it has shuddered through his net—an open gill—the headrope bellying against the flow. He knows the eeled and yabbied holes, the mudeyed snags shimmering with dragonfly. He knows the spawning streams and springs.

All year he is at his nets, cleaving wood for hoops, lifting bark like young skin. Then loop and pull and pass and twist, sheet bend and clove hitch, the twine unfolding from the tongue like a running line. His unlikely fingers flit above the netted air like dabchicks, working the rope and needle. And when the nets are set he feels the drag and pull of water like a familiar caress.

Whatever the stream has spawned or claimed is delivered to him. Each net bulges like a drawstring bag—brown trout, rainbow, yellowed and specked, quinnat salmon, bark and branch. Even when they are all unstaked, packed and folded, he sees them still—forever swelling into a stream of his own imagining.

Top left: *A simple timber house marks the boundary between cleared paddocks and heavy bush at Steiglitz, near Geelong.* Top right: *An early tractor becomes part of the landscape it has worked.* Above left: *Mornings can be chilly in the mountains at Benambra.* Above right: *The ready availability of local timber helps determine the style of shedding and outbuildings at Mansfield.* Opposite: *Early morning light catches the ridges of South Australia's Flinders Ranges.*

WOOD

For sixty years, the valley has heard the whine and gnaw of tooth on wood. Three generations have worked at fell and haul and cut. Blackbutt, messmate, mountain ash, mutton-wood. Thirty acres a year fed to the saw in the split-wood mill. Tree by tree they have shunted them in. Length by length they have dropped. Post and rail. Board and beam. Straight-edged, clean. The new-cut paddocks fenced, the houses framed. The mill itself—setting stumps and throwing up new walls—built of the very thing it feeds on.

Inside, the sawtooth jockeys breathe the wood and work with splinter-ridden fingers. They gnarl and harden. The owner feeds his left hand to the saw and it spiders across the boards, seeking refuge in the pile of strip. He joins the race of quiet men—lopped and stumped, wielding brooms, waiting each day for the saws to stop.

Two years on, the mill will shut for good. No more the rip and tear and thwack of belts. The cleared acres will say nothing, until the new mill opens on the jagged horizon, a sawtooth range already starting on the next town.

Above: *Australia's timber country provides a rich, renewable supply of quality hardwood. Sawmill towns like Tolmie and Swan Reach in Victoria process up to 28 types of eucalypt as well as silver ash and turpentine for building, fuel and cabinet making. Opposite: Cut and stacked timber marks the end of a heavy day's work at Ensay Mill.*

THE PLOTTED LINE

Whether it is fenced or furrowed, ploughed or planted, whether it is ribbed with shining corrugated steel, everything runs straight along the surveyed line. Every boundary is straight-edged, clean, charted by grid and ruler, set and squared as though the rolling hills were flat. Two chains by five to the measured acre—the area a man can plough each day. One man. One horse. One cast-iron tine inscribing corrugations in the broken earth. Each plot has its product, each product yields its price. Everything is answerable to the columned ledger—the debited and credited days of the ordered farm.

The roads run north and south or east and west, dead straight to the flat horizon, washboarded with their own compacted corrugations. Few are cut to the diagonal. There is nothing roundabout round here. The imperial grid has been slapped down regardless of the contoured land. Towns are laid out in ten-chain blocks. Even our states run straight—the shortest distance between two points.

One thing is for certain, you know where you stand on your plotted tract of land. You can take a bead, squint into the sun as you line the future up along it. Look dead straight into the heart.

THE STONEWORK WALL

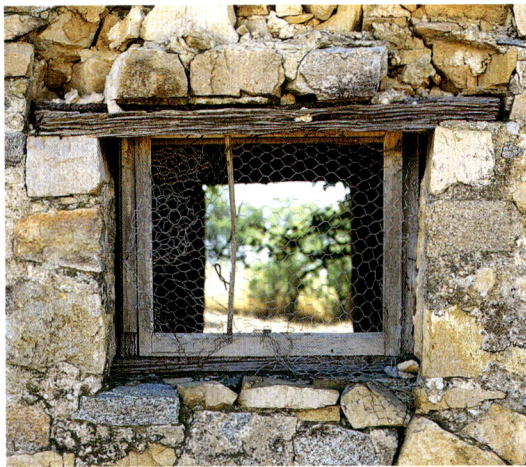

The thing about stone—more than its weight, more than the cold it harbours like the deep—is how accustomed it is to waiting. In creek or paddock or weathered ridge, the perfect block waits to be lifted to its purpose. All it needs is finding. Sometimes you chance upon it, facing blankly from the ground. Other times you search for days, prising unyielding fieldstone from the earth. It is work that can't be rushed. Each stone to its place and time. Haul and gather. Lift and dig. Barrow the findings to the pile. You work by touch as much as sight—reaching instinctively for the cornered stone that fills the gap, the tiestone that will hold a wall intact, the massive ledgestone to be blocked and tackled into place.

A good wall starts well below the ground. It is founded on bedrock, trenched to the frostline then levelled and plumbed. Stone by stone it rises. Course by mortared course it lifts itself above the earth it came from. Each stone locks tight against its neighbour. Granite to slate. Basalt to schist. Creekstone holding to greenstone as each one is puzzled to the wall. Three square feet to the ton. Pound and chisel. Feather and maul. A stone will crack on the third pass, cutting a wedged line as neatly as any saw. Rake each tight joint. Keep each crevice small. The thing about stone is how long it takes to fall.

STACKING THE FLAT ACRES

It starts early, this parcelling up of summer for the months ahead. First light or earlier to beat the heat, with the tractor already ticking in the paddock and the swish and cut and fall of sheaves laid flat.

The carters stumble to it, flexing their backs against its weight and carting the baled hay to the truck. Five days' carting will square the paddock. Cut and bale and twine and stack, like building a wall. Gather the flat acres into compact blocks and pile them each on each. They will still be at it when the paddock is streaked with shadow and the tractor lights are flaring over evening.

All summer the wind moved through it, rippling the grass like water. Now it buffets hard against its mass. Nothing will move it. A well built stack won't budge. See how it throws its own shadow enormously across the land. There is all manner of grass inside it. Oatgrass, barley, clover, rye—whatever has been blown or carried to it by the hayfevered wind of spring and summer. Bidgee widgee, Bathurst burr, wireweed, spear grass, stork's bill, thistle. Things that will open skin or rub thighs raw as the bales are kneed and shouldered to the stack. Pile it high. All around, the same wind prickles across the slashed and stubbled paddocks, bringing with it the unmistakeable smell of rain.

WORK

WORK

TECHNOLOGICAL INNOVATIONS over the last hundred and fifty years have demanded much resourcefulness of rural people. Increasingly, physical endeavour is accompanied by research and sophisticated agricultural practice. Nevertheless, there's no escaping that much rural work involves back-breaking labour that could not be endured by most city people.

During the 19th century, when most of our existing agricultural regions were opened, the patterns of settlement and land use were shaped largely with simple agricultural tools. Great tracts were cleared and turned with axes, cross-cut saws, spades and basic ploughs. Paddocks were fenced, houses built, crops planted and reaped for a good half century before the benefits of mechanisation were fully realised. A man with a scythe could reap about half a hectare of wheat a day. With a simple reaping machine and brace of horses, the same man could do the work once done by sixteen men. Or women. A letter from a Victorian farmer published in 1902 reveals:

'My wife did as much as a man until the youngster arrived. She helped with the clearing; can work a lever with anybody; I've seen her shift a four-foot log and get it in position on the pile. She helped with the fencing. She did most of the 'picking up' on the piece I'm ploughing now. And last year when I am bad with the influenza for nearly a fortnight she went on with the ploughing as well as I'd do myself, the kid in a big box at one end of the paddock watching her.'

Mechanisation, of course, has vastly improved the farmer's lot. It has also increased the range of skills required to operate efficiently on the land. Most agricultural workers today have a knowledge of simple engineering. Most machines are repaired on the farm. Management and agricultural research are as important as the more traditional roles of fencing and shearing. If anything, work on the land today is characterised by its sheer diversity.

A typical working day on an Australian farm might involve fencing, mending the tractor's hydraulics, rounding up stock for vaccination, consulting with agents, mixing chemicals, and attending to accounts. With farms increasing in size and markets constantly diversifying, managers have to be up to date with water management and soil analysis techniques, and be alert to new opportunities. Who would have thought this land of sheep and wheat would be producing essential oils, opium poppies or alpacas?

Itinerant workers also need to be increasingly resourceful. A contract fruit-picker is likely to be an accomplished fencer who can cart hay with the best of them and supplement his income with shooting between seasons. He may also have developed a specialised skill—leather-working, trapping, whip-making, water divining—the knowledge passed on without formal trainee schemes. Even with agricultural training colleges and degree courses, rural work is still heavily reliant on hands-on experience and the advice of neighbours and friends.

The working day starts early and finishes late, its rhythms regulated by the needs of animals and the changing seasons. It might start at five with milking and finish well after dark with the month's accounts spread on the kitchen table. Annual leave and the eight-hour day have little to do with those working the land. The average 'cocky' works sixty hours a week, weekends included.

While it was once possible to keep a farm viable through sheer hard work, changing marketplaces and the unpredictability of world trends means versatility is now the key. Farmers know they need to combine the physical work of breaking the soil with the smart work of research, innovation and good financial management.

THE FARRIER

Thirteen hands or twenty to the withers, they are all four-footed, all need shoeing. Quarter horse, Clydesdale, Waler, hack. All carry their weight on the iron ring. Yearling, stallion, gelding, mare. All stand patiently unbalanced while the job is done.

Here is what you will need. A hammer with a tapered claw. A rasp. A drawing knife to trim the hoof, and pincers. Hoof clencher, pritcheled buffer, twitch. A way with animals won't go astray, a voice as soft as your touch. A steady hand for driving steel to horn. Hold the pastern, press the quarters with your hand, lift the leg across your own and take the weight. Feel the animal twitch and quiver. Feel it breathing at your side. Place the chiselled edge beneath the clench and tap. Pince and prise the old shoe off and let it fall, softly, to the powdered ground.

The new shoe is cold and clean. Draw the knife across the hoof and snip the horn. Rasp and scrape. Bed the metal in and drive the bevelled nails to the groove. Pitch them to the wall inside the thin white line. Let the horse ease the new shoe to the ground, standing straight and squarely pointed. One down, three to go and the next horse waiting just across the way.

THE SPRUNG EARTH

All through the mountains dingoes ran in packs, slinking down from the high plains after dark, moving like shadows, sniffing the wooded air for the sharp scent of metal as they headed for the sheep. Clarrie Lucas stopped them in their tracks. Eight shillings a skin, and a truckful of traps. All along the Timbarra and Dargo rivers he sprung the summer paths, planting the steel jaws like seed. Across to Benambra and down to Bruthen. Up to Mount Nunniong. Wherever there were dogs. He lifted each blade of grass and scraped the earth. He took each root and leaf. Topsoil and stone, clod and clump. Each in a separate pile on his hessian sack. He scooped and hollowed, lifted and scratched, lowered the gaping thing into the hole. Then everything went back in place. He eased his weight from the triggered earth. Nothing to show, nothing to see. Only Clarrie Lucas knew where his traps were set. A clump of grass, a ridge of stone. A detailed map in his knowing head and the patience to wait. Then the lurch and clang and the yelping howl as the ground itself slammed shut. The mountains rang to the sound of them. Every night there was something to claim. Purebreds, crossbreds, great-jawed things that hardly looked like dogs at all. All wrong-footed by Clarrie's traps.

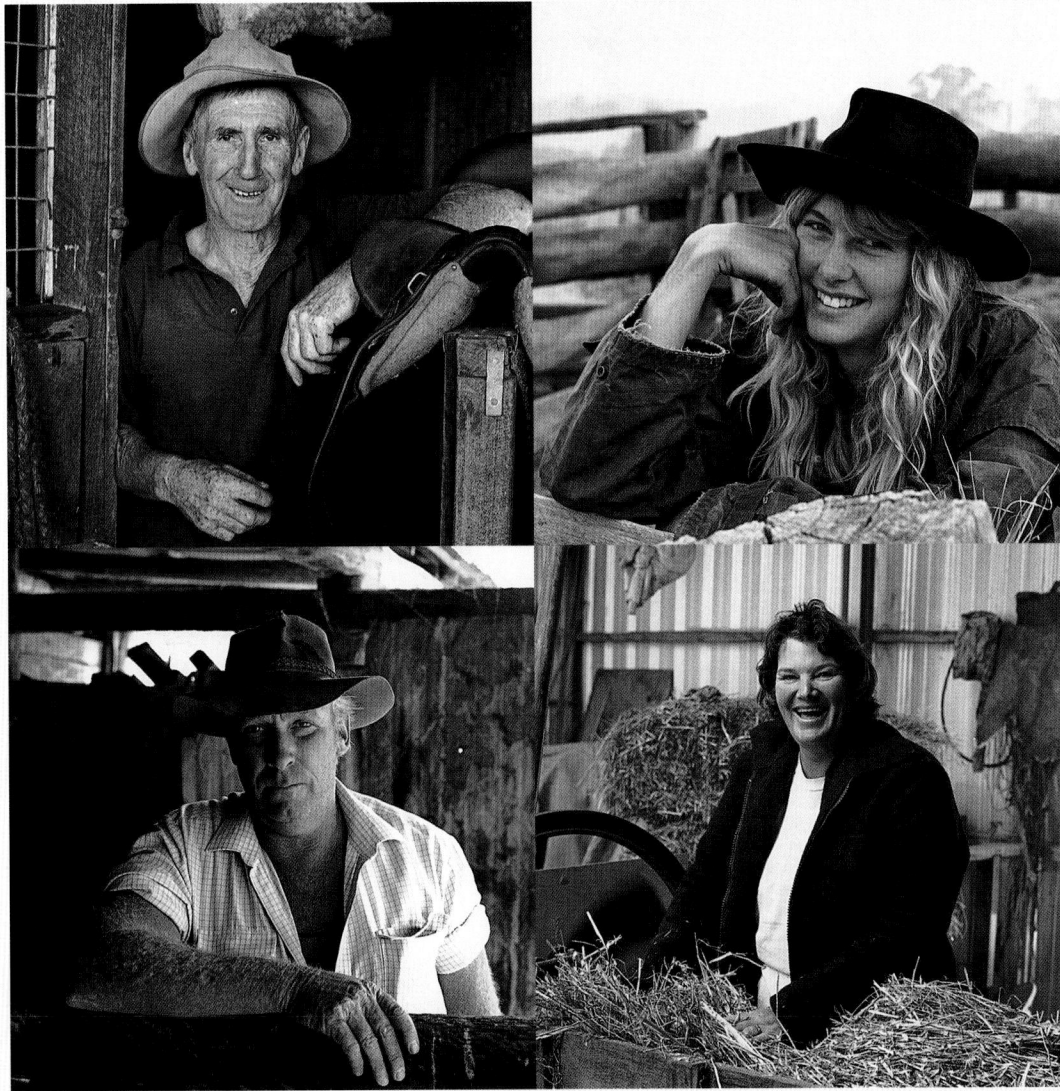

Top left: *Jim Sandy, champion horseman, Buchan.* Top right: *Tammy Carney, Buchan.* Above left: *Derek Martin, fencer, Mansfield.*
Above right: *Glynis Coleman, Benambra.* Opposite: *Debbie Hiscock moves sheep on Reedy Flat Road.*

ANVIL

All day the anvil music rings out from the bellowed shed. Each time the steel-faced block is struck its clear note issues from the throated beak. Each hammer brought against it—ballpeen, shoeing, cat's-head, sledge—brings forth a different sound. Each punch and swage, each drift and chisel forges a new chord in the heavy air. The blacksmith tempers blades for scythes, quenches the beaten steel, hones knives to sharper edges than the highest note. He fills and flattens, crimps and scrolls, pares and rasps—an orchestra of tools laid out about him. Each day he plays the tune his father taught him when he first stepped foot inside the forge; the tune already ringing through his big-boned son.

THE BOARD

Listen to it. Each season it comes to life, sounding a century of cuts through the thick air. It has its own rhythm—the chatter of blades, the hum of cutters. All along the board the picker-up dances through wool. Twenty down-tubes gyrate from the spindle. Twenty gates spring open from the pens.

'Wool-away. Sheep-O.'

Open the belly and nip the points. It's all in the touch, they say—a supple wrist and balanced blade, plenty of lead on the comb. See how the thrown fleece falls flat to the table. The classer fingers its value with lanoline hands then it is armed to the bin to be pressed.

A thousand sheep before the bell, four hundred pounds to the bale. The guns set the pace and the boss of the board keeps tally.

'Broom there. Tar.'

The penners whistle and shove and the expert sharpens the blades.

You can pick a shearer from his hands. One is bigger and softer with knuckles like polished stones—the rouseabout hand—branded with nicks and burrs. The other is calloused and corned. Each season his wrists expand. Long run or short, blades or machine, the hands still give it away. Grab and pull, twist and drive. All day the glorified scissors whisper through wool, all day the two-inch comb lifts for the cut, till the sound of the bell and the satisfactory ache of a job done well.

Top left: *The board in full swing has a hypnotic rhythm of its own.* Top right: *A good shearer works more by touch than sight.* Above left: *Smoko at Tongio.*
Above right: *A double-box Ferrier wool press can press up to 60 bales a day.* Opposite: *Peter White opens the belly with the long blow.*

Above: *Often indistinguishable from play, work is an integral part of a country childhood. Between the routine chores of cleaning boots and helping with the sheep, there is time to take the bikes for a spin across the paddocks or to drop a line into the creek and while away the hours. Opposite: Young helpers take their place in the tray for the rough ride home across the paddock.*

THE LONG PADDOCK

Harold and Ando take them out on the long paddock for weeks at a time, ambling at grazing pace on the wrong side of the fence. All day on horseback, droving the mob along the thin-edged stock route. Everywhere they look is dry except the watery horizon which lifts and swims. Even here there is precious little feed. The docked and spear grassed roadside is specked with broken glass. It is gorsed and thistled, thinly spread. They prod them along to the next dribbling creek and keep an eye for cars.

'You can count on it, no-one for hours until you're crossing them over, then you'll see the dust. Usually it'll be someone you know. Landry, or one of the Michaels boys heading into town. They'll stop and lean out for a yarn, pass the time. There's not much conversation with the stock.'

They are headed nowhere in particular. Out along one side, back the other—the same familiar landmarks in slow reverse—then out again in the opposite direction.

'They'd eat their way from here to Coonabarabran if you let them. They'll walk alright, as long as there's grass to eat. Heads down, mouths open. They don't travel for the scenery. Not like us, eh?'

The horses twitch on the approach to home. Two weeks' travelling to arrive where they began.

THE PLAITED HIDE

Who would have thought the air could crack like that, tearing first like a wet sheet then the sting of it ringing like a shot? All from a piece of plaited hide. See how he brings it back to life, rippling through the sky like a bunched muscle. It loops and buckles, gathers the still air to itself, then opens with a crack like something being snapped—a back perhaps, or glass. All it takes is a languid flick to bring the whole day to that one point. You feel it more than hear it, flinch before the bruised air, eyes snapping shut against the leathered slap. Skin on skin. A sharp punch without the knuckle. The gentle art of breaking. And no sooner is it done than it arcs again, the tapered sinew bellying out, tickling the air with its red-hide tip, then whip, whip, whip, sounding its name with each easy stroke before the fold and crack. Each ear in shot is pricked. All through the quiet hills the day is broken with its sharp retort.

BREAKING THE SOIL

Each year, the paddock opens more easily beneath the blade, the soft earth falling gently from the steel. It folds against itself like a breaking wave, shining with moisture at the cut—a straight, brown wake that doesn't close. The plough trails a cloud of birds as it turns the rich, dark soil to the sun.

By midday, half the hillside will be patterned; its contours etched, each small irregularity erased. Each hour's work will be marked with corrugations. From a distance, you might have combed your fingers through it. How easily it furrows now. How readily it breaks.

Not long before, the ground refused to give. Each compacted metre fought against the share. Each tumbled stone and twisted root jarred the frame until it lifted from the soil and scraped inconsequentially across the hardened surface. Scour and scratch. Drag and stall. The first harrowing line drawn through unbroken earth, then the reassuring feeling of the steel teeth settling in.

TOWN

TOWN

FOR A COMMUNITY DEFINED BY its relationship with the land, the country town has always been held in high esteem. A focal point for people who spend much of their working life apart, town offers an opportunity to meet, catch up on news, and feel a sense of belonging. A proper Australian township in 1892 needed three pubs, a lockup, four churches and a cemetery, according to a Victorian country newspaper. While some settlements grew around ports, mines or railheads, many country towns of the time were little more than developed crossroads. One named its four corners 'education, recreation, salvation and damnation' for the school, sportsground, church and hotel.

Australia's country towns have long since changed. Each has developed a distinctive character through its community and the industries it supports. Each has prospered or declined in response to the discovery of gold or coal, the building of rail links or bypass roads, the relocation of industry to regional centres or fluctuations in world markets. The solid bluestone bank and iron-laceworked buildings of a once-prosperous gold town define its heritage as readily as the weatherboarded dwellings of a sawmill town. An element of truth remains, though, in the 1890s observation. We might need to add a self-serve petrol station and regional library to the list, or a digitally networked information centre, but it is still possible to generalise about what makes an Australian country town.

The Catholic church will stand on the rise, the C of E nearby, most likely with a paddock of no-man's land between. Each pub

will have a back bar and a ladies' lounge recently converted for gaming. One will do gourmet meals; the other will have the sportsmen's bar. The stock and station agent will know everything worth knowing in town. An engineering works down a side street will supply water tanks and small machines. The general store will be a supermarket with wooden floors and the same girl working the register and deli. A hairdresser and barber will complement each other's business.

The post office will be where it always was, a telecommunications tower now prickling behind it. The cinema, long closed, will have been replaced by a video store in the main street. The old bank will serve Devonshire teas and display artwork from the district. There will be an RSL with a World War II artillery piece outside it. The Mechanics Institute will offer distance education. The Masonic temple will open once a week, next to the council chambers.

Beyond the town itself, past the saleyards and agents' offices, there will be a sportsground and pavilion. An old mill, converted for the antique tourist market, will stand beside the butter factory. The road in will take you along the avenue of honour to an arch or obelisk in memory of local boys lost at war.

Australia's country towns are products of generations of necessary change. Some have obviously been more dramatically transformed than others, but all have been influenced by the changing nature of work on the land, the continuing trend towards regionalisation and the increased mobility of the rural population. Town is where the rural community gathers. It is where you find out who needs help and what needs doing. Whether it is the church, the school fete or the pub that draws you in, or simply the need to stock the cupboards and collect the mail, town brings people together.

THE GENERAL STORE

There's not much you can't get at Hogan's General Store, unless it's Burdekin duck or Murrumbidgee jam. They've got Akubra hats and Zulu polish and everything in between. You want some dust for baking, say. There's Whacco, Featherweight, Whoop-whoop or Magpie all stacked out the back in sacks. Sunrize powder if it's dynamite you need. Swallows for biscuits, Sundowner jams. Tea will be Treybon or Robur or Rabbit or Roo. Chokaroo condensed milk, Sunlight Soap. Reel Brand for clothes—'Even a Man Can Do It'. Koala Cola and Football Punch. Possum for paper, Digger's prunes. Eau de Queensland and Num-Ba-Won perfume. There is Spark-O and Go-Poof and Boomerang Tonic; there is Sharkol and Shake-O and Coo-ee and Dog. Ask and they'll find it. If Hogan's don't have it, it's not worth having. Kango and Zebra, Dinkum Digger, Surf. Grippo and Life-Boat, Jello and Clag. Buck-jumpa bacon and 'Huttons is Best', 'Mine tinkit they fit' and 'Hed-Eez for Rest'.

There are Kool-Mints and Murphies at ten for a penny, Jok-Megs and Jaffas and Peppermint Twists. There are Dainties and Euclips and Freddos and Cats. There is Jelicious Jelly, and Tingles and Thrills. There is Tarax and Marchant's and Buffalo Bills.

'Stiffitis for Backache', Heenzo for coughs, Palmer's Pink Powders and Happy Jack Froth. Castle's Paint—'Repaint or Repent', Rat-Menu, Choke-A-Mouse, Cheerio Kerchiefs. 'Dethblo the Insect Foe', Chesty Bond briefs. Rubbagrip, Tarzan's, Fay-Mos and Shore. Australian Maid, Kurrajong, No-Dregs and more, put it all on the slate at the general store.

Above: Country shopfronts in Longwood, Newstead and Clunes hint at the range of goods to be found inside. In the bush, 'store' means what it says—a place to stock up on provisions for the long months ahead. There is nothing quite as tantalising as the rich aromas and the clutter of tins and produce that confront you once you step inside. Opposite: Roma Jenkins, Loch , Victoria.

CAKES AND MILKY TEA

She knew them all when they were boys—the Dalgety's man, the Stock and Station Agent, the mayor and the police—knew them when they were knee-high, scoffing her doughy scones from the trestled table, giving cheek. Now their own children do the same.

How many cakes and urns of tea? How many sandwiches cut and cornered for sales day and the country fair? The young wives, almost girls themselves, ask for recipes, but how to explain a pinch of this, a shake of that, throw sultanas in or raisins? Once word was passed from mouth to mouth over milky tea at kitchen tables, or people simply knew. She has a cake for every occasion. Betty's High-rise, Verna's Boiled Date, the Chocolate Sponge that everyone lays claim to. The Cake of Kisses and the Fruit Loaf from somewhere down near Melbourne. In her drawer at home are two firsts for fancy icing from the Royal Show. And she does a good pavlova.

Her plates are scattered through the kitchens of the district.

'I've still got one of yours, you know.'

'And I've got one of yours,' she laughs.

A touched arm says more than words, kids need minding and a casserole needs leaving by a kitchen door. Her own door is always open, the kettle always on. She knows everybody's secrets but never says a word—all confided over cakes and milky tea.

ALPHA HALL
WEIR'S
ALPHA HALL
Gallery
HOT PIES & PASTIES · FRESH BREAD
Daily
HIMALAYA BAKERY
NEW LIFE BREAD
1P

INK, PINK, PEN AND INK

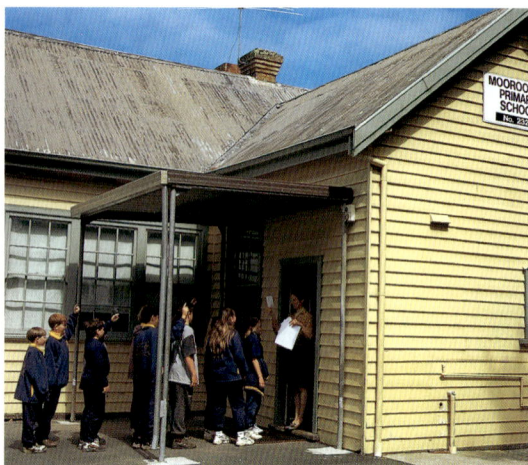

A state school's a great school, it's made of bricks and plaster,

The only thing about it is its baldy headed master.

   I saw Peter kissing Margarita.

I'll never go to school no more, more, more,

There's a big fat teacher at the door, door, door.

   I saw Jack peeking through a crack.

Talking like a two bob watch, all day long,

Talking like a two bob watch, all through the night,

One day his head'll fall off and school will stop.

   I saw Esau on a seesaw.

The teacher and a monkey were sitting on a fence,

The only difference was, the monkey had some sense.

   Tic tac toe, here we go.

Down in the meadow where the green grass grows,

Sits little Jimmy with a marble up his nose.

   White fish, black trout, eeny orey, you're out.

Stink, stink, stink, your mother's in the sink,

Your father's in the dirtbox eating bread and ink.

   Teacher, teacher I declare, give me back my underwear!

THE SAWDUST FLOOR

No place for the squeamish here. Beyond the sawdust floor and sprigged displays—a butcher, butchering. The serious business of leaning into flesh. A quick wink to the farmers' wives then into it out the back. He knows the way a body's strung together. Sinew, muscle, tendon, joint. Knows how to separate each from each. His fingers (all miraculously intact) have slid and parted more meat than he recalls, opening it to the knife, reducing a beast to chop and blade and cutlet for the plate.

Every cut there is, he knows. Loin, shoulder, topside, rump. A knife rattling at his side for every job. All day he cleaves and packs, serving their animals back to them, pounded and ounced from the wooden block. His days are walled with it, boned and carcassed, ribbed and flanked, the heavy sides hung from his hooks like drapes. He shoulders each one to the block, reads its history through its marbled flesh—a lean year here, too long on sorghum—slicing through the seasons with his knife.

And each time the sprung wire door slams shut he is there, wiping his bloodied fingers at the counter, smiling as he calls each customer by name. He knows the way to the heart. Knows who is in for kidney, liver, tongue. A bit of cheek to make them laugh. Always the right piece put aside. Just the thing, he says, and passes the white-wrapped parcel like a gift.

WATERING HOLES

Frank and the ghost knew the town when it was just a pub. 'A pub and a store,' says Frank. 'Tiny and the Star and H.V. and Casser and that lot would come in on their bikes from out along the Devil's River Road and they'd have their sugar bags strung across their shoulders. Old Darmody would rub his hands to see them.'

Frank leans against the bar, looks into his beer.

'It was six o'clock closing then. They shut the doors right on six and whoever was in stayed in. They'd try to leave but Darmody would shout a round. He'd put the money in his own till and they'd have to do the same.'

He laughs at the thought of them locked in for the night with all that beer.

'We were just boys. We'd be outside in Dad's car, six or seven of us and a couple of dogs, and we'd toot the horn and Darmody himself would come out and give us red lemonade to keep us quiet. Taught us how to drink. Some days they'd all be in there. Piddleback and Noxious Weed and Mel and Tibby and the Colonel. They'd be shearing or hay carting for one of the farms and they'd all come in. You'd see them pedalling back home the next day and they'd have their few potatoes and their lard and their corned beef in the bag across their shoulder. But the beer would always draw them back. A good bush pub will always bring them in.'

Above: *Pubs have always followed closely on the heels of the railway and early wool routes. Often, they doubled as changing stations for coach companies and provided welcome relief during long and arduous journeys. While some were rough and ready, others were oases of comfort and gentility.*
Opposite: *Distinctive iron lacework decorates Victoria's Golden Triangle.*

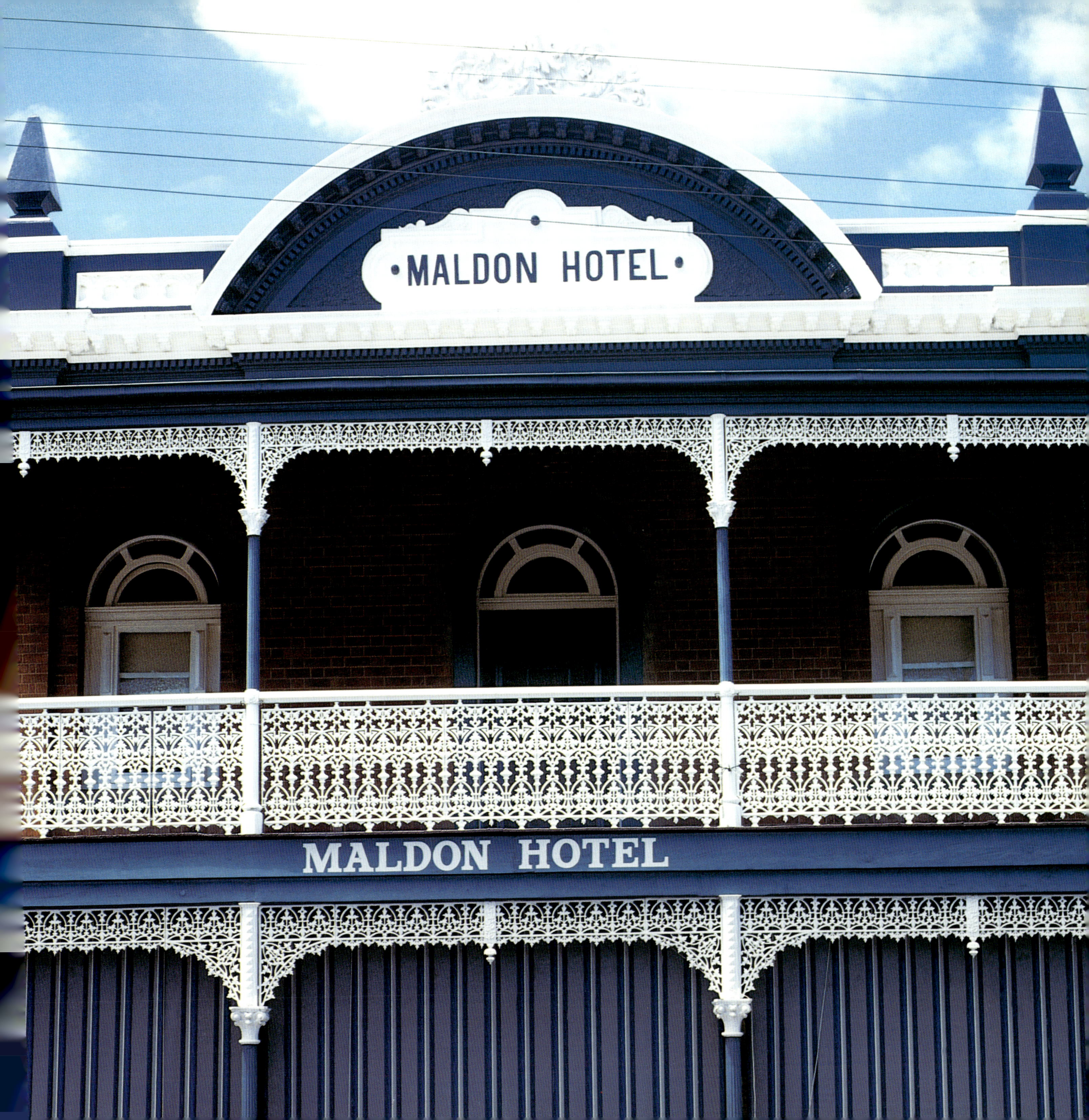

MALDON HOTEL
MALDON HOTEL

THE PUBLIC HALL

Four walls, four corners, a pitched or gabled roof—a wooden box set on stumps at the four-cornered crossroad of the country town. Functional, solid, well-proportioned, neat. The imperial dimensions of Church and State laid out on the rectilinear grid. This is how the landscape has been squared. Framed and battened. Roofed and clad. Double doors opening to the wind of main street. A stage or altar up the back. A tearoom to the side. Folding chairs. The names of the dead, a generation of farm boys lost, in gold letters beside a picture of the Queen. A square can be put to any purpose—church or temple, public hall, education or salvation. Dance or bingo. Cinema or show. No town is complete without one. No hall is complete without a town.

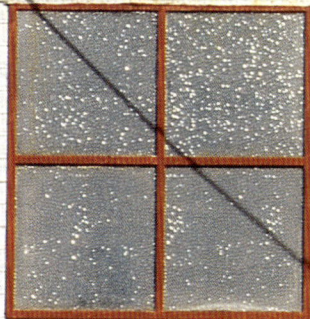

Above: *Often, the most impressive and elaborate architecture in country towns is to be found in the official buildings of church and state. Whether it's a church at Daylesford or the town hall at Tungamah in the Murray Valley, the solid construction of these buildings reflects a long-term commitment, faith in the future and plenty of civic pride. Opposite: Christening a new child brings family and friends together in Bruthen, Victoria.*

CIN
Barambogie
Crystal
NOW
CINEMA
SATURDAY MATINEE
ADULTS
CHILDREN
T.R. SUMMERFIELD & CO
FURNITURE REPAIRED UPHOLSTERED FRENCH POLISHED
COUNCIL CLUB HOTEL
BILLIARDS ROOM
AND SAMPLE ROOM
DISPLAY AREA FOR
SALESMEN

COMMUNICATION

COMMUNICATION

IN RURAL AUSTRALIA, distance has always brought people together rather than kept them apart. You see it in the characteristic wave exchanged by country drivers; in the warmth of country hospitality and the strength of volunteer community organisations in the bush. Nowhere, perhaps, is it more evident than in the bush telegraph, that automatic networking as country people spread the news, especially when someone is in difficulty or need.

Australia's coastline stretches for some 20 000 kilometres, roughly the same distance that separates Australia from western Europe. Its area is not much smaller than that of North America, but with much more open space between towns. Many of the characteristics we have come to recognise as distinctively Australian—resilience, independence, stoic self-reliance coupled with a willingness to help neighbours out—are a response to the sheer size of the country. People always turn to each other for support.

Country people have built their own churches and public halls. They organise volunteer fire brigades and agricultural shows, and band together for entertainment. The lines of communication are always open. Over the years, horse paths and footways between neighbouring farms have developed into a network of roads tying settlement to settlement. Major highways follow the tracks cut by early coach services. Shearers, fencers, pickers and overlanders used these same routes to carry news from station to station. During the 1880s, faced with long journeys and often difficult terrain, rural workers were among the first to embrace the

new rubber-wheeled bike, initiating the transition from horse to machine. Fifty years later, they were quick to recognise the advantages of the motorised bike and car. Mail rounds and public transport routes follow the same roads today. Millions of sleepers and thousands of kilometres of steel have also bound country towns firmly to each other since rail lines were first laid during the 1850s, the shrill whistle and hiss of steam gradually giving way to diesel and electric power.

The first trunk-line telephone calls in Australia were made in 1878, just two years after Alexander Graham Bell demonstrated how the system worked. By 1880, exchanges were established in Brisbane, Sydney and Melbourne. Before long most country towns had their own manual exchange and the party line became synonymous with country life, its very nature reflecting the openness of rural communities. For years, people in outlying regions relied on the familiar voice of the operator to put them through, drawing comfort from the knowledge that kilometres of telephone line, strung between hardwood poles, tied them to each other. Now, radio phones and digital networks provide immediate access both to friends and relations on the far side of the world and to vital information about weather or market fluctuations.

Rural Australians may be connected to the world, but it's the closeness they develop as a community that sets them apart. Whether it is road, rail, radio or telephone that links them, country people look out for each other. Hours spent working separately on the land makes getting together important. Right from the start, the distance between settlements has been compensated for by a deep sense of community and belonging.

THE BROAD-GAUGED LINE

The 5.05 brings the mail, whistling in from Bairnsdale before first light on the sleepered rails, its furnace building up a head of steam to wake the dead. The line is cut and trestled, banked and levelled, holding a steady gradient of one in thirty as it zigzags in.

One hundred and eighty pounds of regulated steam and the glass still filled with water. The engine drags its own weight up the line. A hundred and thirty ton of steel, fifty ton of coal. The dancers on the footplate sweat and shovel while the driver keeps an eye. Six hundred gallons in the tank and water stops all along the line.

You can't mistake its coming. Long before you see its billowed plume you hear it, singing through the steel rail. Put your hand to it and feel. All eighty miles of the spiked and fettled track vibrates with its approach—a small disturbance drawing close. It took two years to get here. Two hundred axemen felling for the navvies, twenty gangers laying ballast for the track. The contoured ground was cut and scoured and gashed. Fifteen hundred sleepers to the broad-gauged mile.

Now it comes in twice a day, ten stops to the railhead, clicking over points. Beside it, the levered wire sends signals up the line, anticipating the first harmonious whistle of the 5.05 on time.

Top left: *A typical country railway station, Avenel, central Victoria.* Top right: *Steam locomotive, Mornington.* Above left: *The age of steam is still alive in Victoria's Dandenong Ranges where 'Puffing Billy' sets out from Menzies Creek.* Above right: *All aboard for the country line.* Opposite: *The power of a locomotive is still evident in the immense steel drive wheel.*

THE MANUAL EXCHANGE

'Getting through? Three minutes. Are you extending dear?' For more than twenty years, Mavis and Fran have staffed the board, keeping the lines open twenty-four hours a day. Eighty town lines, a hundred and thirty partied farms and stations listening in. It is names, not numbers, here.

'We keep them all in contact, let them know we're here. Sometimes all they need's a natter when they're so far out, or else the baby's screaming or someone needs the doc. They ring us and we can ring around, let those know who need to know. Sometimes it's just knowing there's someone here, even if they never lift the phone.'

Each call is clocked and docketed, billed from the regional office down the line.

'Sometimes people will ring in from out of town with messages for shearers or a fencing contractor somewhere miles out, and it's up to us to find them. They'll trust you with that, which is kind of nice. Or the police will tell us that a road's out and we spread the news. City people don't like the party line. They think it's stickybeaking into others' business, but it's not like that at all. It's more like looking out. Seeing who can help.'

'Three more minutes. Are you extending?'

In front of them, a tangle of jacks spilling from the board. They slot them in, send the voices slipping out along the slung lines that loop from pole to pole, tying the community together.

TO CALL...TURN HANDLE, LIFT HANDSET & LISTEN.
TO ANSWER...LIFT HANDSET AND SPEAK.
WHEN FINISHED...REPLACE HANDSET ON HOOK AND TURN HANDLE.

STAMPED AND SORTED

By morning tea he has them sorted, all the paddocked acres chequed and ordered, weighed and pigeonholed in wood.

Adams, Allen, Baillie, Croft. All news passes through his hands. The stamped and sealed, the windowed bills, the missives flown in from daughters overseas, the agent's note, the wool cheque, the letters of foreclosure. He knows more about them than they know themselves.

Forster, Grigic, Grady, James. He slides the catalogue beside the quote, the test results beside the cards. A place for everything and everything in its place. Each name is a farm, a house, a roadside drop beside a twisted gum or where the dirt road meets the tar. He knows the route better than he knows himself. Each day's tidings are bundled to the saddled bag and trotted out. The horse knows where to stop.

Nicholls, Noble, Russo, Wood. Each will make their way to him, winding in to town themselves along the same route, envelopes in hand. Payments, letters, declarations to be signed. Each pushed across the polished counter, passed in confidence to him in the weatherboarded office to start the journey out.

Above: *Roadside letterboxes sprout from the ground near Cassilis in Victoria's high country, revealing as much about the people they belong to as the distance covered by country mail runs. Most are practical and unassuming. Opposite: By contrast, this official receiving pillar, now displayed at Victoria's Coal Creek, reflects all the prepossessing authority of the Crown.*

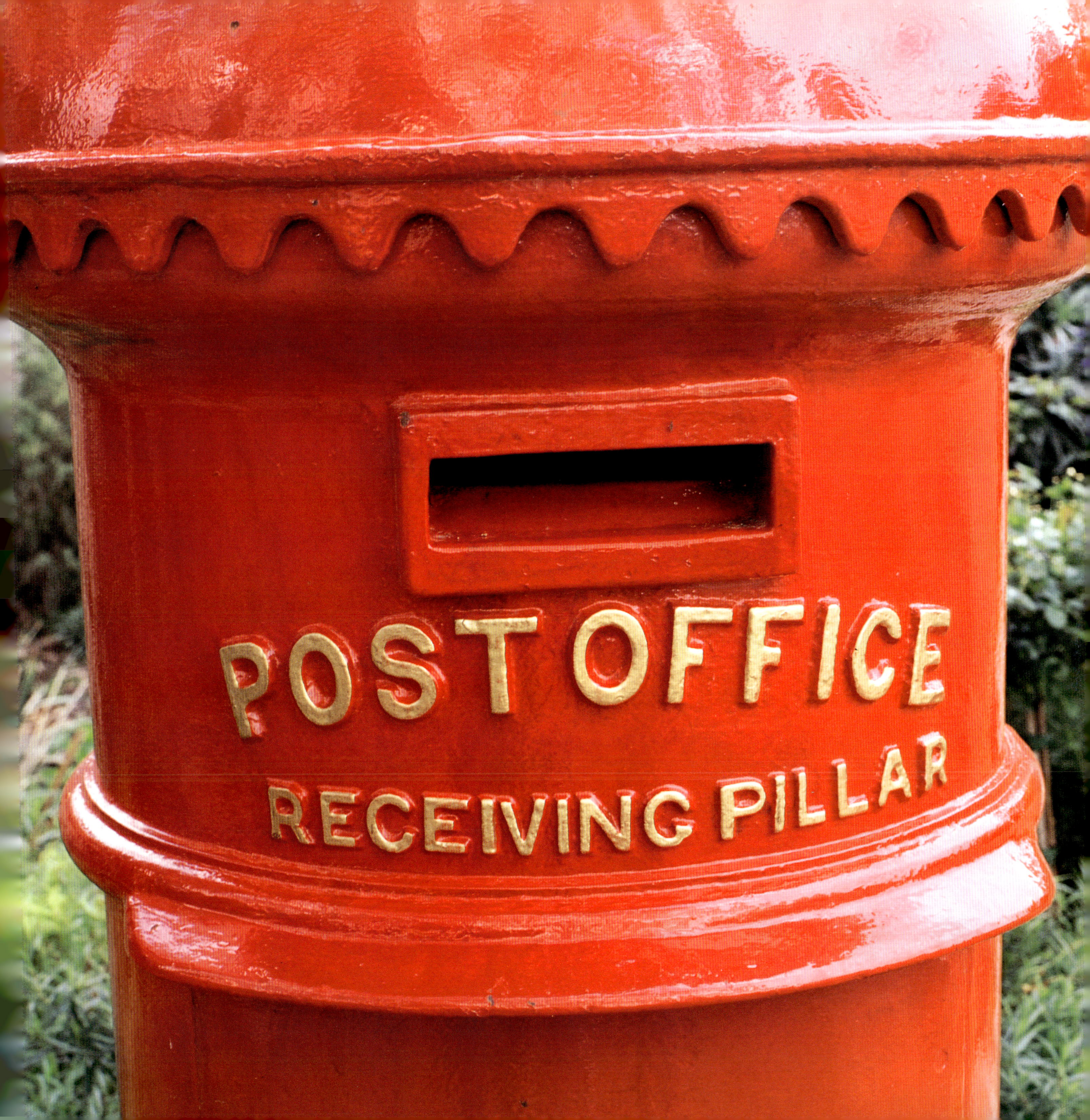
POST OFFICE
RECEIVING PILLAR

THE COACHMAKER

It is more of an art than people realise—keeping the wheels turning and the sprung trap taut. When a road is little more than two deep ruts meandering through trees, the whole machine has to float as much as roll.

Sometimes there is no way through at all but the track the spoked wheel cuts with its banded rim, bouncing from rock to ridge with every turn. The trick, he knows, is to make the hard trip easy, softening the blows with springs and padded seats.

He pulls each strut tight to the long-grained beam—brace and truss, splint and sash—draws the thin-sticked frame together. The axle is mounted to the chassis, the footplate suspended from the rail. Some are built for comfort, others for speed. Some bear heavy weights from town to town. Every turning wheel brings people closer to each other, harnessing the settlements together. Each new coach route brings the mail in quicker; each new carriage reels the distance in.

He'll fix a gig, or float, or buggy; he'll mend a surrey or a brake. Trap or carriage, chaise or brougham, jinker, phaeton, hackery or dray—as long as it is spoked and shafted, the coachmaker knows how it fits together, knows how to send each wagon on its way.

THE CUT AND
CAMBERED ROAD

You can still see the old road running through Grayden's paddock—two deep ruts cut like a scar beneath the winter grass. Come summer, it flowers like an open wound with pimpernel and capeweed from the horse-drawn days. Before that, it was barely a road at all, more a trailing line between flashed trees, sometimes opening to a path. It followed the easiest contours like a creek, winding its way from settlement to station the same way that water finds its level.

A day's ride either way would bring you to a town. Slung on leather straps between the creaking wheels, the coach would sway and swagger like a ship at sea, ploughing through dust to the steady clop and haybreathed smell of horse. Cart and wagon, trap and dray. The shafted jinker rocked on iron rims as it spoked its way back home.

Now, the road cuts a straight line through the hills, finding the shortest route between the towns. A day's drive takes you interstate on the tarred and cambered highway. All that horsepower compressed to the block. Chrysler, Holden, Austin, Ford. The beat of hooves echoes in the thump of pistons. And, for every trough and changing station, a bowsered roadhouse looming through the trees.

HANGING OFF THE RAILS

You will hear it in the yards from Goulburn through to Yea. Different names, different towns, but the same memory filtering through the dust of fifty years or more of sales—of men and stock and the serious murmur of money changing hands.

'Sales day would bring them into town. All the outsiders would come in. The Doyles and Rennies, the Maloneys and the Edwards and Squires. They'd all be in selling sheep and cattle and catching up on news. And Elders and Younghusbands would be there—the agents. They might be looking for a mob of weaners or a bull or something that someone wanted. They'd have a few pots then wander up to the saleyards and have a look and they might start bidding.'

All across the country, the same code of nods and twitching fingers, the scrutinising eye. A year's work hinging on a bid.

'I was a kid then, hanging off the rails. All of us kids would be there, hanging off the post and rail fence and we'd be two rails high and the auctioneer would poke the animals around so everyone could get a look at them. It used to be dust in summer and mud in winter and bulldust all year round. There'd be nods and winks or someone in the crowd would touch their hat, and somehow the auctioneer would know whose bid it was. Afterwards, some of them would be back up for a drink, or they'd stay round the yards yarning for a while. That's when the talk would start—when the business part was done.'

HOME

HOME

THE AUSTRALIAN COUNTRY HOME is characterised by its comfortable informality. People usually come and go by the back door, which is rarely locked; the ubiquitous verandah blurs the boundary between indoors and out, allowing for easy transition between the two; the kitchen with its characteristic warmth and clutter is first stop for the extended 'family' of a working farm. It is where meals are served, decisions made and friendships shared—a meeting place and functional working room.

Much of what sets a country home apart stems from its intimate connection to the seasonal rhythms of a working life. Home is part of work, and the domestic rituals of friends and family enrich the lives of all who step inside. There is always the hum of something going on. Someone arriving or about to leave. A message on the kitchen bench and something being lifted from the stove. The Australian country home is as much a centre of activity as a comfortable retreat from the rigours of the day.

It is not surprising then, that design and decoration have always been determined more by practicality than fashion. The country stove and scrubbed-wood table cater for an endless stream of workers and family members with hard-earned appetites. The cedar dresser in the hallway and boot-rack by the kitchen door might look appealing, but they also serve a purpose.

The distinctive character of the Australian country home has its origins in the early rough-hewn settlers' homes, built with marvellous ingenuity in response to Australia's testing climate. While people in the cities were busy building Georgian boxes more

suited to European conditions, settlers in the country were developing a distinctively Australian style of architecture. Isolation and a shortage of manufactured materials forced them to rely on their own initiative and to use whatever was at hand—timber slabs, stone, earth, saplings and bark. The acacia is still commonly known as 'wattle' from the ease with which its branches could be woven for wattle and daub walls.

Regional variations meant that distinctive styles developed simultaneously across the country—bluestone or basalt houses in Victoria, sandstone in New South Wales, jarrah in the west, weatherboards wherever there was a plentiful supply of timber. The stilted and latticed houses of Queensland were a direct response to a humid climate and a preponderance of termites. The verandah, borrowed from colonial India, proved well-suited to Australian conditions. With the introduction of corrugated galvanised iron during the 1850s, it soon became an essential feature of any country home, throwing a welcoming band of shade around its perimeter.

The early country home also contributed to the marvellous egalitarianism of the bush. In outlying regions, where materials were scarce, the poor selector was on equal footing with the wealthy squatter. Both relied on what could be found and often started their farming lives in houses which were indistinguishable from each other. This same spirit survives today in the no-nonsense attitude of the bush and the understanding that people in the country are united through shared experience. Home is not only home to the immediate family. There's a place at the table for anyone who is there.

THE GARDEN GATE

Everything planted here has come from somewhere else—the rosemary from the Nolans, the lavender from the McGills, the hollyhocks and roses from the Joneses down in Melbourne. Everyone who visits brings a slip or cutting to fill the friendship garden out. A bag of bulbs. A propagated seedling. The bricked path threads its way through privet and plumbago, past the coral tree from Queensland, the azalea from New South Wales, past the laurel carried overland from the west. A piece of everybody's garden inside the gate. The catmint by the water tank from Mary, the gardenia from Aunt Lou.

Strange how everything will take except a gatepost. Plant a gate from somewhere else and watch it warp and sag, the mortised endposts skewing within months. Build it out of local wood instead. Foot and batten, bar and brace. A solid gate announces who you are—Wiltshire cross or Norfolk picket. Swing it open and step inside, feel it spring back squarely into place, the latch catching where it should and settling home.

YOUNG SHOULDERS

His days are as endless as the broad acres he has traipsed for ten summers now, the soil soft against his feet. His face is open as the sky. All work is play. All play an education. He helps with baling, milking, carting—anything a boy can do—melding the rhythms of the farm to himself. He knows each paddock; knows which fence needs mending, which gate sticks, which track the foxes use at night. He knows the age of every animal they own. Already, the land has given him the characteristic squint, as though he is lining up his future.

Each morning he rises with the sparrows. Hail or shine, he swaggers out, anxious not to miss a minute of the day. He can smell rain two days before it comes. 'Old head on young shoulders,' they say. 'Weatherwise.' It is as though he has grown from the land he stands on—barefoot, smiling, ready to take anything it offers in his lengthening stride. Ten summers on, he will still be here, and ten years after that, walking the paddocks that claim him even now.

TANKWATER

All is well when the tanks are full, each ring sounding the same dull note as you listen, ear cocked, for the tapped water to announce its level. Higher and higher you play the scale, each knock registering the same satisfying lack of music.

There are eight hundred gallons of it suspended beside the house—three tons—casting a ribbed shadow like a watermark on the boards. Turn the tap. The water continues its interrupted descent from sky, to tank, to ground. Listen to it pitch. Cupped to your mouth, it is cold and sharp with the taste of sky still in it. It whistles through you, spilling like a stream from your hands.

They say a tuning fork will find it. Out in the summered paddocks when the tanks are dry, the steel prongs sound for water. No noise, but a trembling quiver in the still air. A slight vibration transmitted like a signal saying, 'here, beneath the stubbled grass'. Feel it, the gentle tug of a current streaming beneath you to a body of water floating in earth. Plumb it and the flow is reversed—ground water springing to the surface, rising inch by inch to the steady rhythm of the pump.

THE WOOD-FIRED STOVE

There is a trick to it, learned early in country kitchens—first light or before—when the house is still and the birds are yet to stir. Here is how it is done. Open the kitchen door and step outside. The dog will rattle his chain in greeting. Look out across the frosted paddocks. Cup your hands and blow, then take the split kindling from the stack and step inside again.

Open the firebox door—quietly, gently—feeling its cast-iron weight against your hand, then peer inside the heart. There is warmth there still. The banked embers from the night before smoulder in the dark. Open the dampered throat and see them glow. Rake the grate and tickle the vent. Watch the updraft draw them back to life. A wisp of smoke rises to the shelf. Place each splintered stick, an offering, and shut the flanged door tight. You will hear it first, a low grumble rising through the flue, then feel it, the warmth unfolding like a blanket through the house. Poke and jiggle, stoke and vent. Regulate its breathing. All day long it will pump out heat.

Now, fill the kettle from the tank. Bring the cold metal to the hot and listen to it hiss. Punch the dough and work your fingers through it. Knead and pummel, roll and knock. Feel it stiffen as you work. Lift the boiled water to the pot and pour. Watch the cut leaves swell and let them draw. Strong black tea for when you slide the tinned loaves in and wait. Forty minutes in the wood-fired stove, then tap and turn them to the rack.

Above: *Practical household implements, bought when needed, reveal as much about decorative tastes as the domestic realities of rural life. Often the bedroom and kitchen were the only places women could combine beauty with usefulness. Water jugs, porcelain bowls, vases and jardinieres—in many cases imported Doultonware—were cherished possessions. The open pine dresser is not only practical but allows decorative crockery to be displayed.*
Opposite: *Floral designs, transfer-printed prior to glazing, were popular in Australian-made porcelain and earthenware.*

THE KITCHEN

Everyone finds their way here, the warm heart of the family home. First thing every morning and again at night, they gather to it, drawing the comfort of the room about them. It seems the oven never empties. Someone is always pouring tea.

It is here the big decisions are made. In times of crisis or celebration—whenever there is a problem to be figured—the family gravitate towards it, their places waiting for them at the kitchen table. It is where confidences are shared and friendships forged, where the serious business of talking begins. All important things will start or finish here.

You can read a family's history from its kitchen table. Each pit and scratch is a record of their past. Each mark recalls an incident, each wine-glass stain a meal. There is a hollow where the teapot sits, a scorch from the baking dish brought too quickly from the stove, an ink-stain leaching from the wood like a shadowed bruise. Two perfect stiletto circles, just off centre, show where the eldest daughter's dress was hemmed. A deep gouge down one side marks where the carving knife slipped against the bone.

For all the scrapes and polishes the table has received, two generations of homework are still imprinted on its grain. Each cheque written is recorded. Each letter to relations carves another year of news into the scribbled wood.

More than any other room, the kitchen holds the family's stories. It is where you come to talk and eat and laugh and cry. Step inside and know you are home. Friends and family always enter by the kitchen door.

SOUNDING THE BLOCK

Hear it—the solid thunk of the axe head dropping home into the redwood block, the split of kindling opening along the grain. There is music to it. The cadenced fall of wood. The axe swings like a metronome, hollowing out the layered years with its cross-hatched score. Each blow splinters and sticks, each split stacks the pile. A whole winter of wood drawn from the summer thinnings.

The block itself stands firm. Not just block but stool, log, table, chock—any purpose it can be put to. Shoeshine, fulcrum, axle, weight. It has seen three axes out. Two generations have cut their teeth on it, testing its strength against their own. They have clambered, tilted, rolled and kicked, struggled to lift its weight. They have had their first uncertain blows glanced back, barking against their shins to show who's boss. A sharp lesson by the kitchen door. Respect. Perseverance. Strength. And, once a month, a feathered neck outstretched for an unexpected blow. The solid thunk of the axe head dropping home.

Above: Many early kitchens and laundries were furnished with unsophisticated implements of metal, wood and pottery. Much of the metalware was shipped from England, although local adaptations like the Coolgardie meat-safe and the ubiquitous billy soon took on the status of Australian icons.
Oppposite: Late afternoon light catches the twin gables of a South Australian stone house.

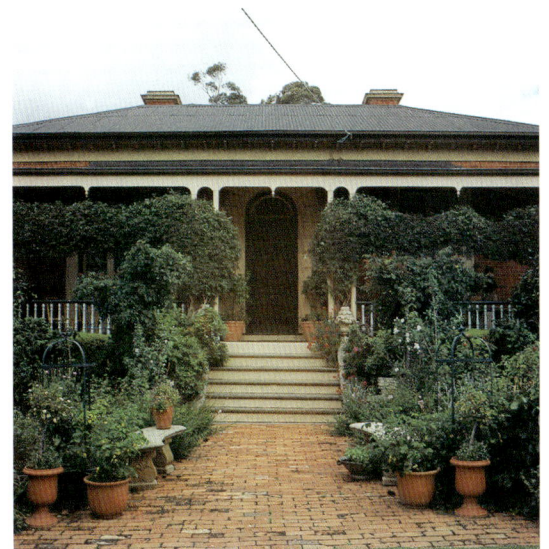

CAPTIONS